INDUSTRIAL RAILWAYS OF SEAHAM

A.J. BOOTH

INDUSTRIAL RAILWAY SOCIETY 1994

© A.J. Booth 1994

Published in 1994 by the
Industrial Railway Society at
13 Trinity Avenue, Bridlington,
East Yorkshire, YO15 2HD

ISBN 0 901096 81 4 (hardbound)

ISBN 0 901096 82 2 (softbound)

All track plans drawn by Ian Lloyd

Printed in Great Britain by
AB Printers Limited
33 Cannock Street
Leicester LE4 9HR

This book is copyright under the Berne Convention. Apart from any fair dealing for the purpose of private study, research, criticism, or review, as permitted under the Copyright Act 1911, no portion may be reproduced by any process without the written permission of the publisher.

Contents

page

Location Plan	4
Introduction	5
Seaham Harbour Dock Company	6
Dawdon Colliery	50
Seaham Colliery	60
Seaham Training Centre	70
Seaham Wagon Works	74
Vane Tempest Colliery	78
Appendices	92

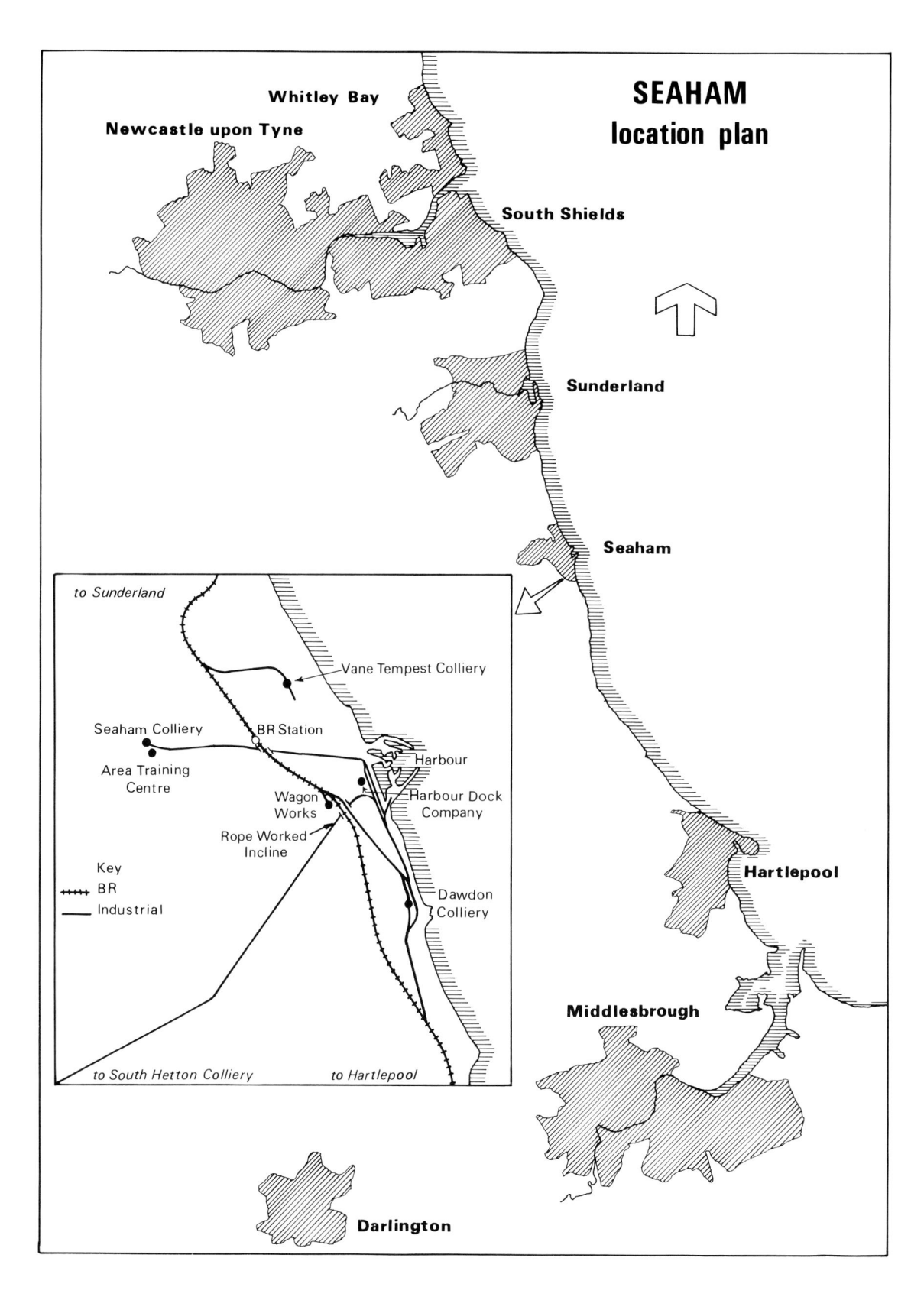

SEAHAM
location plan

Whitley Bay
Newcastle upon Tyne
South Shields
Sunderland
Seaham
Hartlepool
Middlesbrough
Darlington

Inset

to Sunderland
Vane Tempest Colliery
Seaham Colliery
BR Station
Area Training Centre
Harbour
Wagon Works
Harbour Dock Company
Rope Worked Incline
Dawdon Colliery
to South Hetton Colliery
to Hartlepool

Key
++++ BR
—— Industrial

Introduction

Seaham. The very mention of the town's name is enough to produce sighs of nostalgia among industrial railway enthusiasts. Situated on the north east coast of England, a few miles south of Sunderland, the town had three collieries, two inclines, a wagon works, and an NCB training centre; plus an antiquated harbour dock featuring staithes, steam paddle tug boats, ancient wooden wagons, and the country's oldest active steam locomotive. Truly an industrial paradise!

The Seaham Harbour Dock Company is held in affection by many enthusiasts. Not only did the Company operate a particularly interesting railway system, but their staff were always friendly and co-operative in allowing visits. My first was on Friday 29th August 1969 when I saw the veteran Lewin for the first time. I was hooked and, despite dieselisation, have made pilgrimages ever since. A typical visit involved pottering around the harbour, following the 'Lewin tracks' along the breakwater to the lighthouse, watching operations on the rope-worked incline, and photographing the shunting. During the lunch break there was time to sit on the loading bay (see page 37), while the English Electric diesels ticked over alongside, and eat sandwiches which were washed down later by a pint at the 'Duke of Wellington'. Heady days!

In the time before the dreaded 'Health and Safety at Work' regulations the National Coal Board was always prepared to allow visits to their five establishments in the town. It was pleasant to visit the mines and be safely shown round by a typically friendly Durham miner. I had a particular affection for the wagon works where old rolling stock was shunted by antiquated motive power. And is it just a quirk of memory, or did the sun *always* shine at Seaham?

On my most recent visit to the town, on Sunday 16th January 1994, it was a totally different scenario. Not only was it snowing but two diesels, stored unused for eighteen months at the dock, were the town's only locomotives. Dawdon and the Wagon Works were flattened, whilst Seaham and Vane Tempest collieries were in the process of demolition. Seaham as I loved it had gone. The walk along crumbling tracks out to the lighthouse seemed especially poignant, and brought memories flooding back.

Hopefully this book will stand as a permanent reminder of the town's industrial railways. It is intended as a photograph album and not a major history, and readers requiring further information are particularly referred to 'Industrial Locomotives of Durham' by C.E. Mountford and L.G. Charlton (Industrial Railway Society 1977); 'The Londonderry Railway' by George Hardy (Goose & Son 1973); 'Private Owner Wagons of the North-East, volume 1, The Chaldrons' by John A. Elliott (Chilton Iron Works 1994); and 'Seaham Harbour, the first 100 years, 1828-1928' (privately published by authors Tom McNee and David Angus, 1986).

In compiling this book I have received much help from my railway friends and I wish to thank: Ian Lloyd for his painstaking map drawing, in particular his masterpiece of the harbour dock system; Colin Mountford and Bob Darvill who checked the text; Horace Gamble and Colin Mountford who provided information; Mrs Kath Bates who typed the manuscript; and the following who supplied photographs - John Bell, Ian Carr, Richard Casserley, Derek Charlton, John Cowburn, Horace Gamble, Colin Gifford, Tom Heavyside, Frank Hornby, Frank Jones, Kevin Lane, Colin Mountford, Robert Pritchard, and the late Brian Webb. Thank you all.

Adrian Booth
Bridlington

22nd August 1994

SEAHAM HARBOUR DOCK COMPANY

The Seaham Harbour Dock Co Ltd was formed in 1899 during the reorganisation of the industrial interests of Lord Londonderry, the docks being treated separately as their projected extensions required an Act of Parliament. Four locos were transferred to the new company, of which their best known was number 18. It is seen on 16th October 1965 heading along the breakwater towards the new lighthouse which was commissioned in 1905. *(I.S. Carr)*

Seaham Harbour Dock Co. 1956

NORTH PIER
Londonderry Office
NORTH DOCK
OUTER HARBOUR
Lighthouse
to Seaham Colliery
Level Crossing
Tunnel
Office
Loco Shed
Loco Workshop
Lock
SOUTH DOCK
Level Crossing
Coal Staithes
Timber Yard
SOUTH PIER
Seaham Iron Foundry
Rope worked incline to South Hetton Colliery
School
Housing Estate
BR to Seaham
to Dawdon Colliery
Allotment Gardens
BR to Easington   BR to Dawdon Colliery

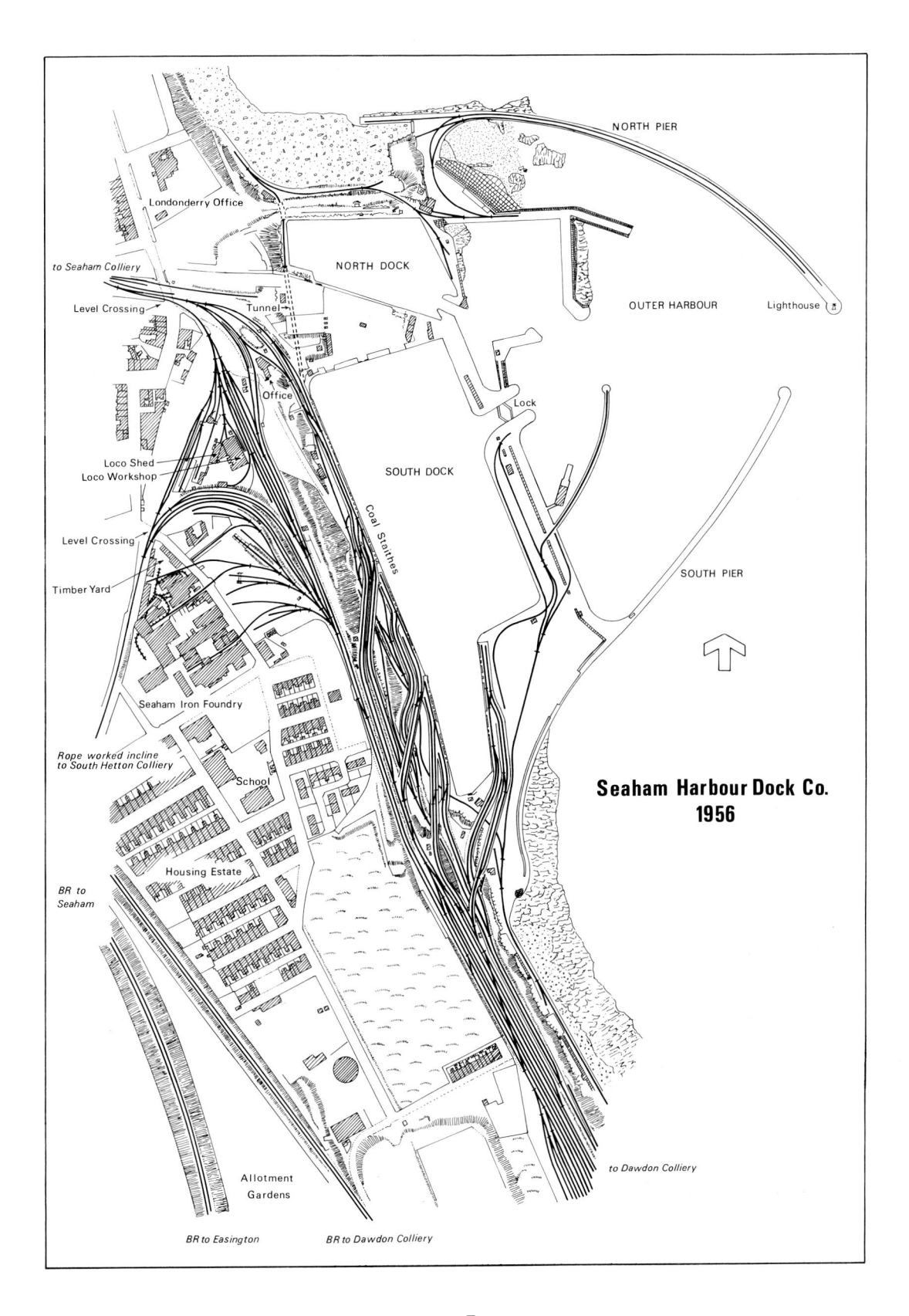

S. Pearson & Son Ltd constructed the new south dock for the Harbour Dock Company. It was commenced in 1899 and was officially opened by Prime Minister Balfour on 11th November 1905. Note the contractor's loco, centre left; the temporary track on the curved wall; and the original 1836 lighthouse, top left, which became disused after the building of the new lighthouse in 1905 and was demolished in 1940. *(collection F. Jones)*

Sadly, the railway out to the lighthouse is no longer used for harbour wall repairs. The rails were deteriorating badly when photographed on 4th November 1985. *(A.J. Booth)*

The 3rd Marquis of Londonderry, a powerful and autocratic coal owner, built the original harbour to ship coal mined at his Durham collieries. Opened in July 1831, the harbour gates were opened by ropes operated by this beam engine built in 1827 by Hawks & Co of Gateshead. It continued in use until 1947 and was photographed on 19th July of that year.
(L.G. Charlton)

Seaham Harbour operated the UK's last paddle steamer tug boats. RELIANT (built in 1907) and EPPLETON HALL (built 1914) both continued in use until 1969, with the former making the very last tow in April of that year. Fortunately both these graceful vessels have been preserved, EPPLETON HALL in San Francisco and RELIANT at the National Maritime Museum at Greenwich. They are seen awaiting duty in June 1965. *(C.T. Gifford)*

The demise of the paddle boats did not signal the complete end of steam in the harbour. CHIPCHASE, a conventional steam tug, laboured on for a few more years and is seen on 9th May 1978, minutes before a sea fret obliterated the scene. *(A.J. Booth)*

The south dock was an amazing sight with a forest of staithes, all rail served. Full wagons discharged their coal through bottom doors and down chutes into collier boats waiting in the dock. This view was taken on 30th June 1978, shortly before demolition. *(K. Lane)*

Thomas Richardson & Sons of West Hartlepool built this loco, works number 254, in 1855. Originally an 0-6-0, it was rebuilt at Seaham as a saddle tank in 1876 and was one of the locos taken over by the Dock Company from Lord Londonderry. *(collection F. Jones)*

Acquired from Londonderry in 1899, loco number 16 was a vertical boiler tank built by Head Wrightson of Stockton-on-Tees in 1870. Despite its antiquated appearance it was useful for dock side duties, on which it was engaged on 30th April 1952. *(H.C. Casserley)*

Number 17 (Head Wrightson of 1873) was also ex-Londonderry, and is seen working beneath the staithes on 19th May 1956. Both the Head Wrightson locos were acquired by their builder for preservation. *(J.E. Bell)*

This delightful 0-4-0 saddle tank (Black Hawthorn 203 of 1871) was acquired from Rainton Colliery Co Ltd in 1903 and scrapped early in 1939. Note the interesting wheels.

(R.H. Inness)

ABOVE: the famous number 18 locomotive was built in 1877 at the Poole, Dorset, foundry of the legendary Stephen Lewin. Built as an 0-4-0 well tank, it was rebuilt at Seaham as a side tank with enclosed cab, whilst in 1927 it was converted to a saddle tank. As built the loco had 9in x 18in cylinders, and 2ft 6in diameter wheels on a 5ft 0in wheelbase. It *may* be Lewin works number 683. It remained active until the early 1970's and owed its longevity to being small enough to squeeze through the low level lines beneath the staithes and through the small harbour-side tunnels. Its primary duty was helping with the periodic repairs to the breakwater walls (built to protect the inner harbour), as on 16th October 1965. *(I.S. Carr)*

RIGHT: in a scene which could almost be from the Victorian era the Lewin trundles a couple of ancient chaldron wagons down to the low level sidings, in June 1965. The chaldron wagon was named after an old standard measure of coal in the north east, and they are synonymous with Seaham harbour where these wagons were 4 tons capacity. Because of their livery they were widely referred to as 'black wagons'. One is now preserved beside the Dock Company's main gate, and there are others at Beamish Museum and at the Bowes Railway.
(C.T. Gifford)

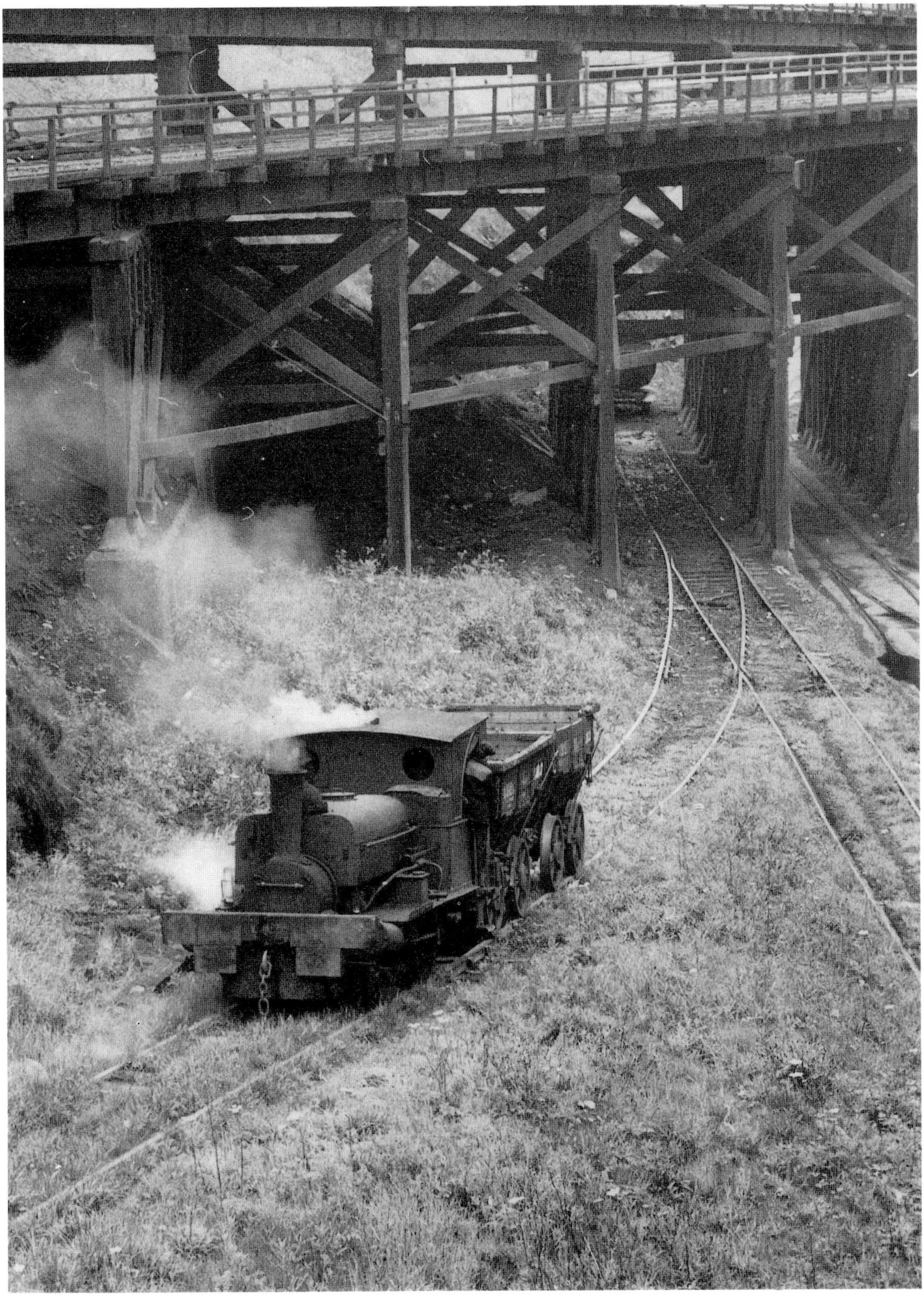

A portrait of the Lewin at Seaham on 2nd October 1965. Compare the number plate with that of number 19 on page 13. Note the sharply inclined cylinders, a feature of this builder's locomotives. Number 18 is now preserved at Beamish Museum. *(J.E. Bell)*

The Dock Company never had a proper numbering scheme and at one time had two number 18's. The second was Black Hawthorn 32 of 1867, purchased from the NCB and seen on 19th March 1963, nine months before it was scrapped. *(C.E. Mountford)*

A scene which epitomises the Lewin, as it squeezes through the north dock tunnel in June 1965. The abandoned trackbed and tunnel mouth can still be viewed today. *(C.T. Gifford)*

MARS (Robert Stephenson 2238 of 1875) hauls a rake of chaldron wagons. Sadly this fine engine was scrapped in July 1963. The L on the chaldrons is a throw back to the Londonderry Railway.
(L.G. Charlton)

Another view of MARS, illustrating the curved lines of the cab and the nameplate. She was under repair on 30th April 1952. Note the handlamp, and the chalked comment 'won't move' on the back right buffer!
(H.C. Casserley)

CLIO was built in 1875 at the North Eastern Railway's Gateshead works, and was acquired from them in 1911. She was scrapped in 1955. *(L.G. Charlton)*

CLIO's tender on 30th April 1952. The loco was in pieces on this date (its cab can be seen in the lower photograph on page 28) and it is doubtful if it was ever reassembled.
(H.C. Casserley)

MILO (Robert Stephenson 2241 of 1875) was sister to MARS, and was in steam on 30th April 1952. She was scrapped at the same time as her sister. Note the lengthy line of chaldron wagons in the background. *(H.C. Casserley)*

REX (Manning Wardle 838 of 1885) worked for Pearson on the south dock construction illustrated on page 8. Acquired in 1905 from the contractors, she was scrapped in 1939.
(collection F. Jones)

There was no steam loco shed at the harbour and locos were always scattered around in the open. DICK, a quaint Hunslet (works number 628) of 1895 vintage, is seen on 19th May 1956.
(J.E. Bell)

SEATON carried its nameplate to the left of the cab entrance and a worksplate 'Seaham Harbour Engine Works 1902' to the right. Note its twin buffers. It is seen at the harbour on 22nd May 1957 with Sentinel TEMPEST in steam in the background. *(L.G. Charlton)*

The Dock Company purchased two new 0-6-0 saddle tanks from the manufacturers, Peckett's of Bristol. The first was 1052 of 1905 named SEAHAM, seen here on 8th May 1960. It was scrapped in 1961. *(L.G. Charlton)*

The second Peckett was 1083 of 1906 named SILKSWORTH. It gave 57 years service before being cut up in July 1963, but was in steam in April 1958. It was another loco with twin buffers, for shunting both conventional and chaldron wagons. *(F. Jones)*

44 (Manning Wardle 1934 of 1917) was an 0-6-0 side tank purchased from the NCB in February 1960, but it was not a success, being scrapped in July 1963. It was awaiting its fate in the Dock sidings on 19th March 1963. *(C.E. Mountford)*

The South Durham Steel & Iron Company of West Hartlepool sold a pair of Hawthorn Leslie saddle tanks to the Dock Company in November 1961. No.1 (3354 of 1918) is seen in August 1963, six months before scrapping. *(F. Jones)*

No.3 (Hawthorn Leslie 3355 of 1918) was the second ex-South Durham Steel & Iron loco and continued the trend of unsuccessful buys, being cut up in 1967. It was photographed in August 1963, with a welder on the cab roof. *(F. Jones)*

Hawthorn Leslie 3352 of 1918, seen here on 12th June 1965, was another short lived loco. Purchased from Dorman Long's Acklam Works, Middlesbrough, in June 1963, it was scrapped in March 1967.
(H.A. Gamble)

B No 10, Hawthorn Leslie 3476 of 1920, came from the Consett Iron Company in March 1960. It was photographed on 12th June 1965 and met its fate in December 1966.

(H.A. Gamble)

Another of the Hawthorn Leslie fleet, B No 38 (3496 of 1921). Also from Consett, it lasted seven years before being scrapped in 1967. It was working on 21st October 1964. Note the assorted oil cans on the footplate.

(L.G. Charlton)

Action at Seaham in August 1966 as one of the Hawthorn Leslies makes hard work of its load of steel hoppers. Note the supplementary coal which half obscures the view through the cab window and the coal shovel tucked into the handrail. *(C.T. Gifford)*

B No 23, Hawthorn Leslie 3744 of 1929, lasted seven years after its arrival from Consett in May 1960. It was active on 7th July 1965, with the two man crew peering from the cab as they pose their charge.
(L.G. Charlton)

A fine study of JUNO (Hawthorn Leslie 3527 of 1922) on 30th April 1952. CLIO's cab is on the left, while the important oil drum on the right needs three 'gaffers' to move it.
(H.C. Casserley)

NEPTUNE, Hawthorn Leslie 3898, was purchased new in 1936 and, when photographed on 4th December 1955, still had over eleven years service to offer. A tarpaulin gives the crew protection from cold sea winds. *(L.G. Charlton)*

The quartet of Hawthorn Leslies on these two pages is completed by 173 (3919 of 1937) at Seaham on 12th June 1965. Ex-Dorman Long, Acklam Works, Middlesbrough, in June 1963, it was scrapped in September 1967. *(H.A. Gamble)*

This locomotive's identity is obscured in a cloud of steam and smoke during energetic shunting operations in August 1966. Note the white warning panels. *(C.T. Gifford)*

B No 41 (Robert Stephenson & Hawthorns 7016 of 1940) was obtained from the Consett Iron Co in May 1960. Three loco crew attend to their charge's coal and water needs on 8th May 1960, hopefully obeying the notice (top left) which reads 'on no account must fires be drawn nor ash pans cleaned near this coal stage'. *(L.G. Charlton)*

Robert Stephenson & Hawthorns 7036 of 1940 arrived in November 1963 from Dorman Long, Britannia Works, Middlesbrough, and was photographed on 12th June 1965. It was yet another short stay resident, being scrapped in June 1967. *(H.A. Gamble)*

Dorman Long also sold Robert Stephenson & Hawthorns 7340 of 1946, which lasted three and a half years at Seaham. It is seen in August 1963, two months after arrival. Note the worksplate high on the cabside, the large block buffers, squat chimney, and the lack of side rods and nameplate. *(F. Jones)*

A murky Seaham day reveals 24 (Robert Stephenson & Hawthorns 7342 of 1947) in a sorry state, dumped out of use. Number 52 stands behind. *(collection F. Jones)*

Robert Stephenson & Hawthorns 7347 of 1947 was photographed on 24th May 1967, only seven months before going for scrap to W.F. Smith Ltd of Seaham Harbour. *(J.M. Tolson)*

Double-header action at Seaham in June 1965 as steam and smoke obscures the locos blasting past the interesting little shunting signal. The loco on the right is clearly a product of Andrew Barclay, and is probably Dawdon Colliery's WYNYARD as illustrated in the lower photograph on page 55.
(C.T. Gifford)

Sentinel of Shrewsbury demonstrated this 4 wheel vertical boiler tank loco (9575 of 1954) in 1956 and the Dock Company purchased it two months later. Photographed on 8th May 1960, it was scrapped in 1965. *(L.G. Charlton)*

TEMPEST (Sentinel 9618 of 1956) was purchased new and was pristine on 27th April 1957. In 1959 it was sent to Thomas Hill (Rotherham) Ltd where its chassis was utilised during rebuilding as a diesel, as illustrated on page 39. *(J. Clewley)*

The nearest the Dock Company got to a steam loco shed was the workshops on the left of this 7th July 1965 view. What an interesting yard to explore, with locos, wagons, chaldrons, and cranes on view!
(L.G. Charlton)

What a contrast! The same view on 3rd August 1983, as an English Electric peeps from the shed which had been provided with the advent of diesels. Note the remains of the steam coal/water stage at left.
(A.J. Booth)

ABOVE: this small steam rail crane was standing in a corner of the Dock Company's yard on 21st October 1964.
(L.G. Charlton)

LEFT: the ravages of the sea has done its worst, and even the Lewin and team would be hard pressed to repair this breach in the breakwater railway system! 10th April 1981.
(A.J. Booth)

Dieselisation of the Harbour Dock Company's railway took place in 1967 when five 0-6-0 hydraulics were purchased from English Electric Ltd of Newton-le-Willows. The new quintet pose for their official photograph, with D4 (on the right) delivered the opposite way round to the other four.
(English Electric)

The view from the single road diesel locomotive shed on 26th June 1979. D1 stands in the yard as D3 pulls past with a rake of NCB coal hoppers. *(A.J. Booth)*

On 25th August 1970 three locos pose beside the diesel shed: English Electrics D1 and D5 at left, with Thomas Hill 104c on the right. The latter has lost its 'Vanguard' knight on horseback plate, as seen in the view below. *(I.S. Carr)*

Thomas Hill 104c was a rebuild of Sentinel 9618 illustrated on page 34. Comparison is difficult, but the forty-five degree angled block buffers, and chassis, provide the clues. 25th April 1961. *(L.G. Charlton)*

D1 (English Electric D1191 of 1967) engaged in shunting operations on 9th May 1978. It was scrapped in October 1988. Note the roughly applied SHD Co lettering, extreme left.
(A.J. Booth)

D2 (English Electric D1192 of 1967) holds up Dock road traffic on 4th November 1985, as D3 stands in the background. The Dock Company's gatehouse can be glimpsed, extreme right.
(A.J. Booth)

D2 hauls a string of eighteen NCB coal wagons past the south dock on 11th September 1986, with an unidentified banker at the rear. Note remains of the staithes above the second wagon. Sadly, D2 was scrapped in October 1988. *(J. Cowburn)*

The townsfolk of Seaham were well used to rail traffic between Seaham Colliery and the harbour holding up proceedings. The flagman stands in the middle of the road to guard D3's progress on 4th November 1985. The old 'gaffer' and his dog look unconcerned, while the bill-poster on the extreme right has more important things on his mind.
(A.J. Booth)

D3 (English Electric D1193 of 1967) on 4th November 1985. She was sold to Scottish Grain Distillers Ltd of Cameron Bridge, Fife, in September 1989. *(A.J. Booth)*

D4 (English Electric D1194 of 1967) stabled outside the diesel shed on 8th April 1984. Its Railway Executive registration plate is beside the steps, lower right. *(A.J. Booth)*

D4 has acquired an 'S' logo on its bonnet as it runs light engine past NCB coal wagons on 9th May 1978. All diesels were in green livery at this time. The Harbour Dock Company's offices are top centre.
(A.J. Booth)

D5 works its way along undulating track towards Seabanks signal box, on 30th June 1978, with Dawdon Colliery coal hoppers. The two-directional shunting signals are of interest.
(K. Lane)

D5 (English Electric D1195 of 1967) poses near the loco shed on 4th November 1985, in a later livery of dark blue and yellow. *(A.J. Booth)*

Latterly the Harbour Dock Company also shunted steel for export emanating from Teesside. Sadly, this traffic was lost about mid-1992, and on 16th January 1994 the town's last remaining locos (D4 and D5) lie disused, but hoping there will be a renewal of this traffic.
(A.J. Booth)

Londonderry Collieries 20 ton wooden wagons numbers 170 and 213 stand at Seaham Harbour on 30th April 1952. *(H.C. Casserley)*

Wooden 16 ton hopper wagon 3504 in 'Mebonite red oxide' livery, on 9th May 1978. The lettering to the right of NCB reads BR-NE 12-77 NCB3, with 12-77 being the repair date and NCB3 identifying the owners as NCB No.3 Area. *(A.J. Booth)*

Wagons 3161, 722, 3262, 3064, 3127 (back) and 3229, 3004 (front) on 9th May 1978. Note the disused staithes in the background. *(A.J. Booth)*

An embankment ran round behind the loco shed area giving access to the foot of the rope-worked incline to South Hetton Colliery and Hawthorn Combined Mine (and originally Murton Colliery). Empties await the rope on 9th May 1978. *(A.J. Booth)*

Hopper wagons start the climb to Cold Hesledon and on to Hawthorn and South Hetton on 26th June 1979. This route was opened in 1833 and featured two self acting inclines, Hesledon No.1 (Stony Cut) and No.2 (Swine Lodge). It carried coal to the harbour, but from the mid-1960's was used purely for taking spoil down to Dawdon where it was dumped into the sea (see page 58). The incline was used right up to the 1984/85 miners strike, but as a direct result of coal being dug from the embankment during the dispute the line had to be abandoned, and all track had been lifted by October 1985. *(A.J. Booth)*

A five wagon set (two wooden and three steel hoppers), loaded with spoil bound for Dawdon Colliery, descends the self-acting incline on 25th August 1970. Note the British Railways coast route bridge at top left.
(I.S. Carr)

DAWDON COLLIERY

The first sods for Dawdon Colliery were cut on 26th August 1899 by Theresa Marchioness of Londonderry and her son Lord Castlereagh. Old blast furnaces which occupied the site were cleared away and the colliery was opened in 1907. It was situated on Nose's Point, to the south of the harbour, and its coal seams ran out under the sea. A rail link connected it to the Harbour Dock Company system, whose locos helped shunt their traffic. This was superseded by BR operated 'merry-go-round' trains from 10th August 1987, but the pit closed on 11th July 1991. In happier times 60 (Hunslet 3686 of 1948) stands at Dawdon on 28th August 1974. She formerly worked on the Lambton Railway which featured some tight tunnels, hence the loco's rounded cab.

(G.T. Heavyside)

Dawdon Colliery 1959

BR to Seaham and Sunderland

to Harbour Dock Co. lines

Gantry

Weighbridge
Coal drops

Paddock
Stables
Loco shed

Spoil tipping points

BR to Easington

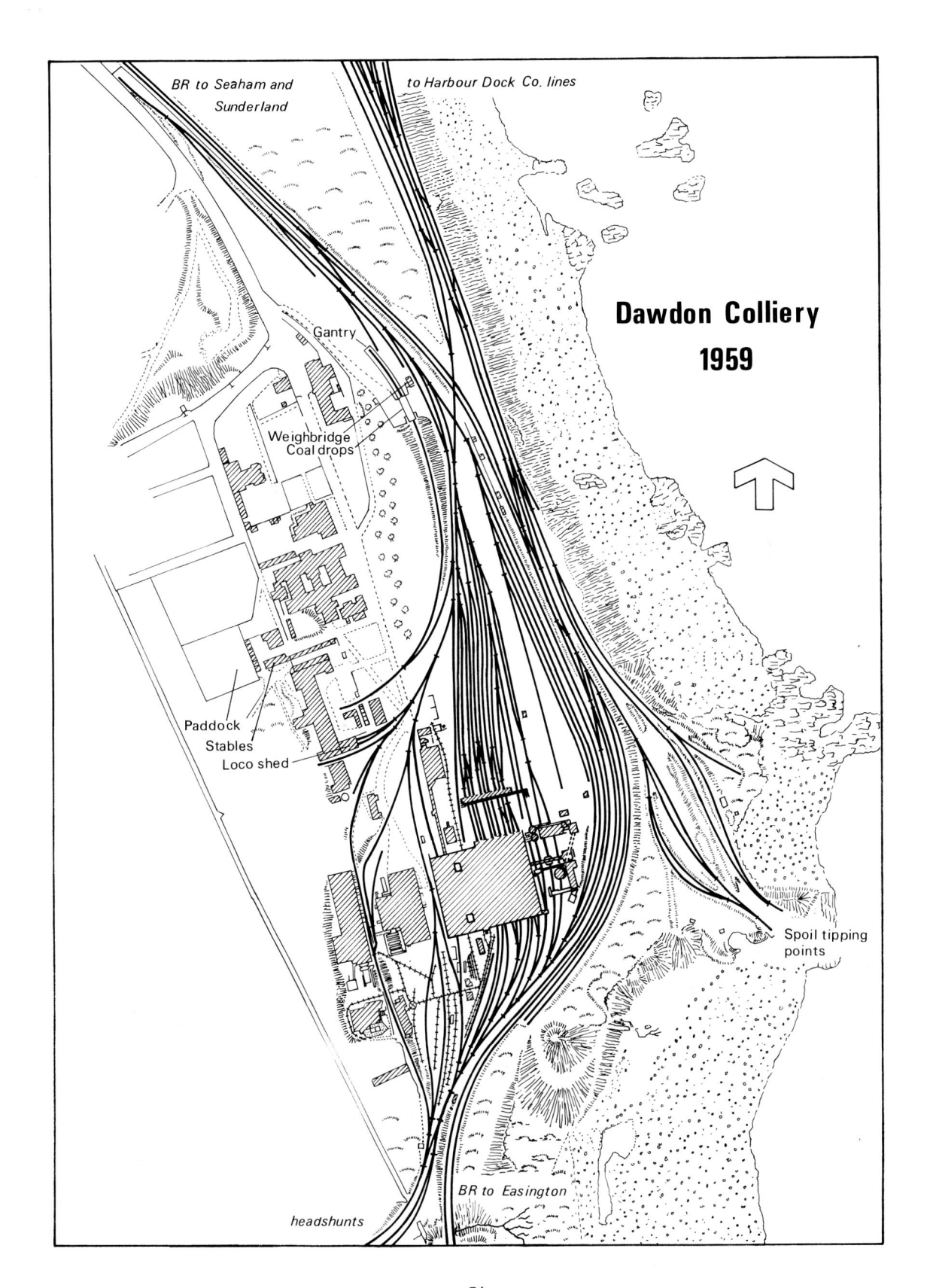

headshunts

Dawdon Colliery in 1934. An 0-6-0 tender engine stands just above the conical heap in the foreground; whilst another stands alongside the signal box and gantry on the extreme centre right. Note the five arch Dawdon viaduct above, and slightly to the left, of the pit headgears. *(Aerofilms 45922)*

11 (Hudswell Clarke 1412 of 1920), seen at Philadelphia in April 1954, later worked at Dawdon. Note the worksplate on the sandbox, a typical Hudswell Clarke feature.
(F. Jones)

12 (Hawthorn Leslie 2789 of 1912) poses for the camera at Dawdon Colliery, with the crew in jovial mood. Date unknown. *(collection A.J. Booth)*

DAWDON No.2 (Hawthorn Leslie 3492 of 1921) at Dawdon Colliery on 8th April 1959. Note the supplementary block buffers for shunting chaldron wagons in the background, and the ornate hut chimney. *(L.G. Charlton)*

Manning Wardle 2035 of 1924 is seen at Lambton Staithes, Sunderland, in June 1952, but was transferred to Dawdon Colliery in May 1964. *(F. Jones)*

87 WYNYARD (Andrew Barclay 2165 of 1944) in steam at Dawdon Colliery on 20th April 1955. It was named after Wynyard Hall, owned by the Marquis of Londonderry until recently. Chaldron wagons form a familiar backdrop. *(L.G. Charlton)*

Hunslet 3686 of 1948, attached to 'tender' wagon number 132, energetically shunts a heavy rake of full coal hoppers on 25th August 1970. She is now preserved at the Strathspey Railway, Aviemore.

(I.S. Carr)

Carrying 'NCB South Durham Area' lettering, internal user guards van No. 7 was parked in Dawdon Colliery yard on 9th May 1978. *(A.J. Booth)*

Dawdon Colliery's brick-built two-road loco shed, on 9th May 1978. The sign between the doors simply reads 'Locomotives'. Note the long wall-mounted hooks for holding open the shed doors. *(A.J. Booth)*

Dawdon Colliery waste disposal point on 9th May 1978. Wagons discharged their spoil here which was taken via the conveyor (right) and tipped over the cliff edge, to be taken away on the next tide. The winch (right) pulled each wagon in turn from the one-capacity headshunt.
(A.J. Booth)

Ex-underground 70hp loco (Hunslet 4110 of 1952) worked for a short period on Dawdon's surface narrow gauge system. It is seen at Blackhall Colliery on 10th May 1978, in yellow livery with red coupling rods.
(A.J. Booth)

400hp 0-6-0 diesel hydraulic, Andrew Barclay 609 of 1976, stands alongside Seabanks signal box on 9th May 1978, working from Dawdon Colliery. She was painted navy blue with red coupling rods, and yellow/black buffer beams. *(A.J. Booth)*

D5 from the Harbour Dock Company positions 36 empty 'merry-go-round' wagons at Dawdon Colliery loader on 4th November 1985. *(A.J. Booth)*

SEAHAM COLLIERY

Seaham Colliery was perched at the top of the town, some two hundred feet above sea level. It opened in 1859 and was struck by a terrible explosion on 8th September 1880 when 164 men and boys and 180 pit ponies were killed. It was linked to the main line by a NER half mile branch, and to the Harbour Docks by a rope-worked self-acting incline, the two running parallel for much of their lengths. Seaham pit officially merged with neighbouring Vane Tempest Colliery from 19th February 1982, Vane Tempest coal thereafter being wound at Seaham. All traffic over the incline ceased from 17th July 1987 when British Railways took over responsibility for all coal and spoil traffic, and the incline was lifted in January 1988. The colliery is seen on 3rd August 1983.
(A.J. Booth)

Seaham Colliery 1956

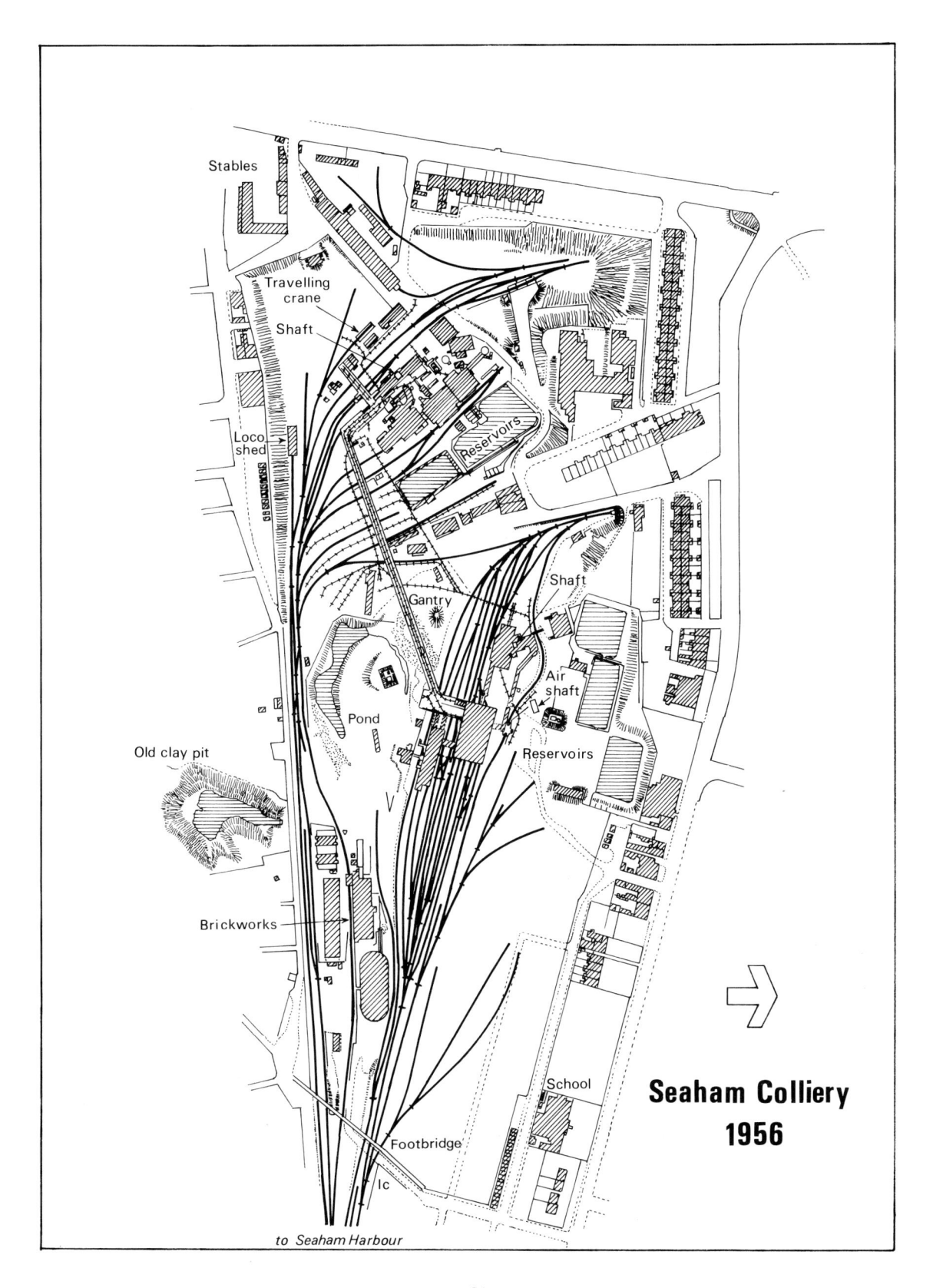

Andrew Barclay 1321 of 1913, formerly of Easington Colliery, had its wheels out at Seaham Colliery on 16th July 1968, shortly before being scrapped in April 1969. *(B. Webb)*

Grant Ritchie & Co of Kilmarnock built this neat saddle tank in 1920 (works number 769), seen on 12th June 1965. She was scrapped in February 1967. *(H.A. Gamble)*

LONDONDERRY (Andrew Barclay 1724 of 1922) pulls a train of coal hoppers through the colliery yard on 24th June 1965. She was scrapped in March 1968. *(C.E. Mountford)*

Hawthorn Leslie 3544 of 1923, its worksplate removed from the sandbox, arrived at Seaham Colliery in April 1965 and is seen here on 16th July 1968. *(B. Webb)*

STEWART (Andrew Barclay 2160 of 1943) stands outside Seaham Colliery loco shed on 24th June 1965, two years before scrapping. The loco was named after Charles Stewart, 3rd Marquis of Londonderry. *(C.E. Mountford)*

Robert Stephenson & Hawthorns 7756 of 1953 at Seaham on 16th July 1968. Compare this loco with 3544 (illustrated at the foot of page 63) built thirty years before. *(B. Webb)*

Robert Stephenson & Hawthorns 7756 shunts eight empties for the colliery, seen top left, on 10th August 1966. The three-rail top section of the incline down to the harbour is seen bottom right, with the wire rope laid alongside the left hand rail.

(R.N. Pritchard)

Andrew Barclay of Kilmarnock were quite successful in marketing their diesels to north east collieries. Works number 523 of 1967, a 233hp model in navy blue livery, at Seaham Colliery on 3rd August 1983, five months after its arrival from Philadelphia. The cabside plates are Rail Executive 1407 of 1953 (upper) and Philadelphia Workshops 1979 overhaul (lower). The erroneous cabside number should have been applied as 2333/241. *(A.J. Booth)*

The locomotive shed at Seaham Colliery on 3rd August 1983, the six side windows long bricked up. Two Barclay diesels were standing within. *(A.J. Booth)*

From 1965 locos were allowed to work the incline (right) and it was singled and the rope removed in 1968. Andrew Barclay 548 propels empties up-grade to Seaham Colliery on 30th June 1978. *(K. Lane)*

At the bottom of the incline on 4th November 1985 Barclay 623 was pushing empties bound for Seaham mine. The 'Duke of Wellington' public house is on the left, and the tracks in the foreground run to the view on page 42. *(A.J. Booth)*

Barclay 623 engaged in shunting operations at the foot of Seaham incline on 3rd August 1983. 623 was transferred to Seaham Colliery on 23rd June 1981, and carried British Railways registration plate NC45. *(A.J. Booth)*

Seaham Colliery on 13th June 1988 with British Railways Class 56 locomotive number 56118 bringing in a rake of 'merry-go-round' empties. *(A.J. Booth)*

The Seaham/Vane Tempest Combine closed for 'mothballing' on 23rd October 1992. Both were soon demolished, however, and this photograph shows the scene on 16th January 1994, the day after the headgear was blown up. Compare this view with page 60. *(A.J. Booth)*

SEAHAM TRAINING CENTRE

The National Coal Board operated a training centre on part of the Seaham Colliery site. Men were trained to drive underground locomotives and received a pass certificate, thereafter attending for a 'refresher' every three years. Enclosed buildings (left) simulated underground loco roadways; while outside tracks (right) gave compulsory gradient and speed retarder practice. The surface system was reorganised in the winter of 1986/87, but due to the drastic contraction of coal mining a central training facility became uneconomic. It was closed on 30th August 1991 and demolished, with training decentralised to the remaining pits. The centre is seen on 3rd August 1983. *(A.J. Booth)*

NCB Seaham Area Training Centre 1983

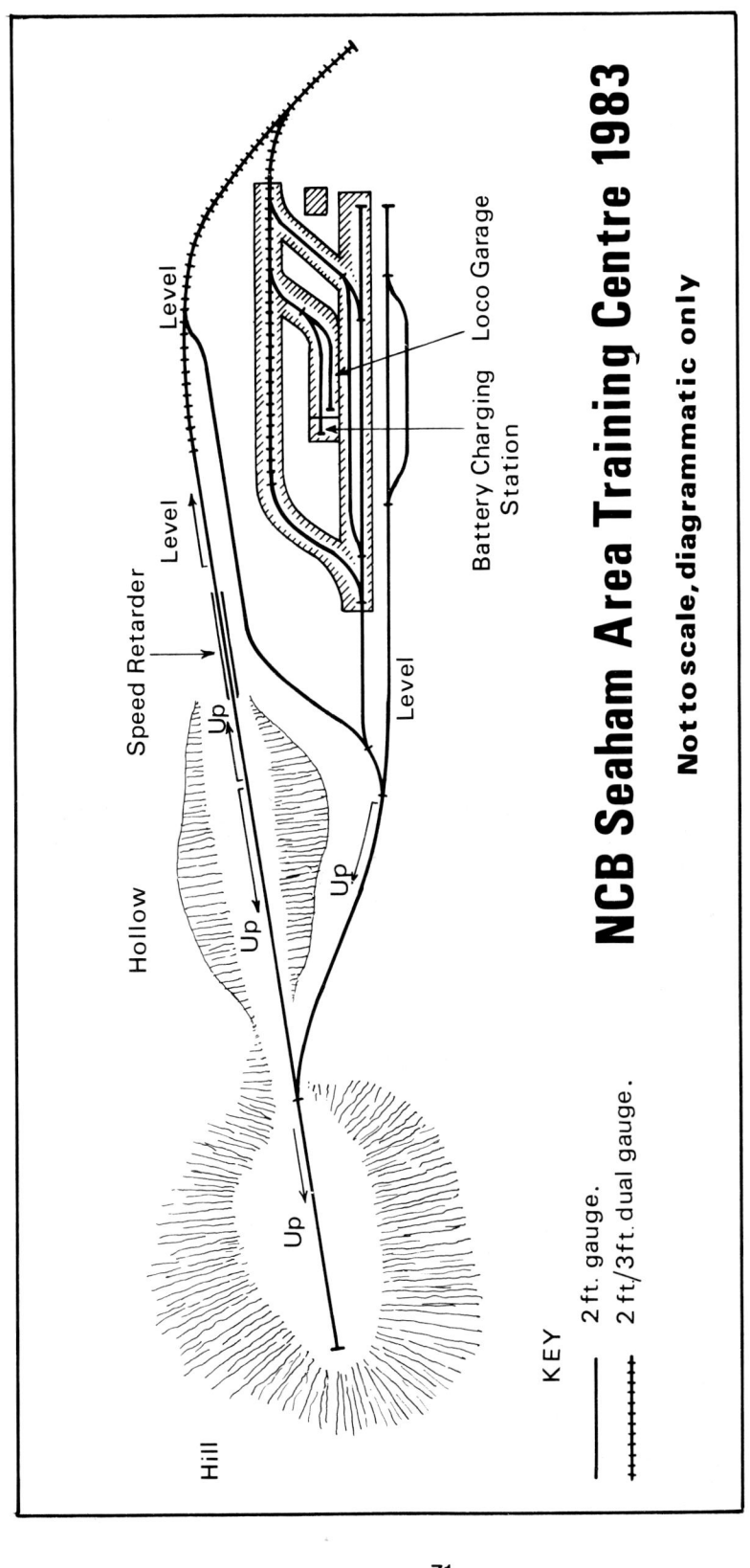

Not to scale, diagrammatic only

Labels on diagram: Hill, Hollow, Speed Retarder, Level, Level, Level, Up, Up, Up, Up, Battery Charging Station, Loco Garage

KEY
— 2 ft. gauge.
┼┼┼┼ 2 ft./3 ft. dual gauge.

Layout of the Training Centre at 3rd August 1983, drawn by Ian Lloyd. Note the dual-gauge track, installed because certain locomotives from other pits, for example Easington, went here for trials/testing. It was compulsory for the speed retarder to be experienced by every driver, as these were installed in most pits following the underground runaway at Bentley Colliery, Doncaster, in 1978 when seven men were killed.

Double-ender 66hp jackshaft drive flameproof locomotive (Hunslet 6619 of 1966) on 3rd August 1983. It was in white livery with yellow/black striped ends. *(A.J. Booth)*

Hunslet 6620 was a 1970 rebuild of Hunslet 5596 of 1961, and was photographed on 3rd August 1983 standing in one of the training galleries. It was in white livery, with yellow ends and red coupling rods. *(A.J. Booth)*

An underground loco shed was universally known as the 'loco garage'. Resident in the Training Centre garage on 3rd August 1983 were English Electric 2519 of 1958, a single ender type EM1-A2 battery electric loco (left); and Hudswell Clarke DM842 of 1954, a white livery single ender jackshaft drive 100hp mines type diesel (right). *(A.J. Booth)*

SEAHAM WAGON WORKS

The year of construction of the Wagon Works is not known. It was located on the west side of the NER Seaham to Hartlepool line, half a mile south of Seaham station. Londonderry Collieries originally owned the works, although wagons from the Seaham Harbour Dock Co Ltd were also repaired here. It was vested in the NCB on 1st January 1947, ultimately being closed on 20th March 1987 and later demolished. It was shunted by horses until 1939 at which date a petrol loco was obtained (see page 76), the start of unusual motive power at the site. This general view of the works was taken on 26th June 1979. *(A.J. Booth)*

Seaham Wagon Works 1957

↑

to Seaham and Sunderland

lc
lc
Goods yard

Housing Estate

Housing Estate

School

NCB to Seaham Harbour

to Dawdon Colliery

Allotment Gardens

Rope Worked Incline

to Easington

BR / NCB
to South Hetton Colliery

1979 layout

to BR

Repair Shop

Paint Shop

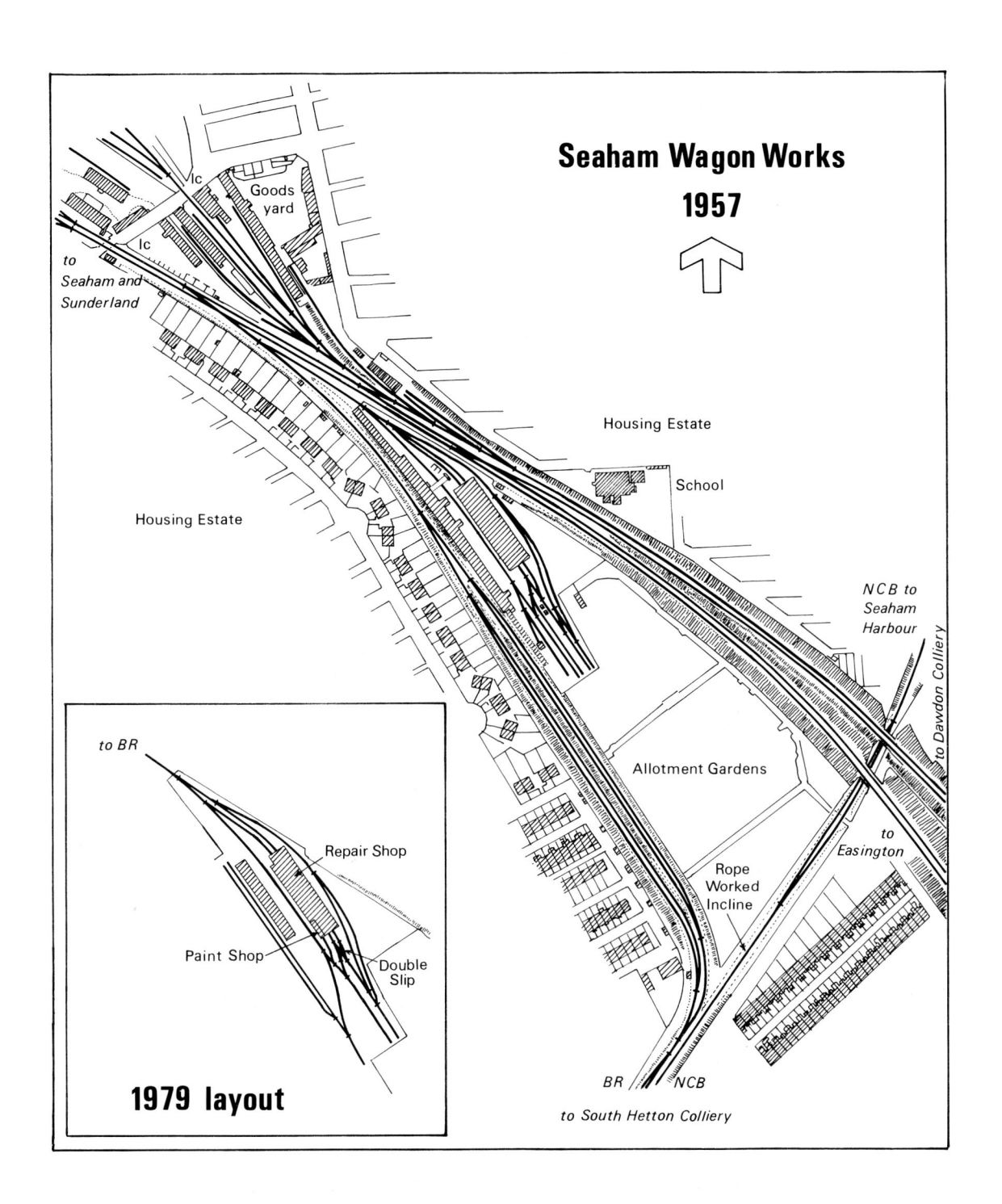

Double Slip

This amazing machine was built by Muir Hill of Manchester (works number L116 of 1939), and was derelict at the wagon works on 28th May 1970. Note the block double buffers, strange wheels, and the tarpaulin driver 'protection'. It was scrapped in February 1971.

(C.E. Mountford)

The Muir Hill was joined by something even stranger! This diesel mechanical was created at the NCB's Lambton Engine Works in 1955 utilising parts of an Aveling Barford dumper. Photographed in action on 9th October 1964, it was scrapped in September 1970.

(B. Webb)

Looking more like a 'proper' locomotive, chain driven Motor Rail 5766 of 1963 poses in the yard on 26th June 1979, in a livery of green with black frame and red buffer beams. Note the maker's 'Simplex' motif plate on the bonnet. *(A.J. Booth)*

Motor Rail 5766 positions a wooden NCB wagon on 26th June 1979. Note the fire extinguisher on the cab back, and the BR semaphore signal extreme right. *(A.J. Booth)*

VANE TEMPEST COLLIERY

Opened in 1929, and built on Londonderry land, Vane Tempest Colliery was named after Lord Vane Tempest, the title of the Marquis of Londonderry's eldest son. It was located close to the cliff top, to the north of the harbour, and its coal seams were out under the sea. A half mile branch connected the pit to the Sunderland to Hartlepool main line, half a mile north of Seaham station. It merged with Seaham Colliery on 19th February 1982, after which coal winding ceased here and its production went underground to be wound at Seaham. It was mothballed on 23rd October 1992 and closed on 7th May 1993, being demolished in 1994. The headgear is seen on 9th May 1978. *(A.J. Booth)*

Vane Tempest Colliery 1958

- Sludge beds
- Reservoirs
- Cooling tower
- to Town Centre
- to BR
- Shaft
- Sludge bed
- Coal drops
- Ramp
- Colliery Welfare Ground
- Shaft
- Loco Shed
- Housing Estate

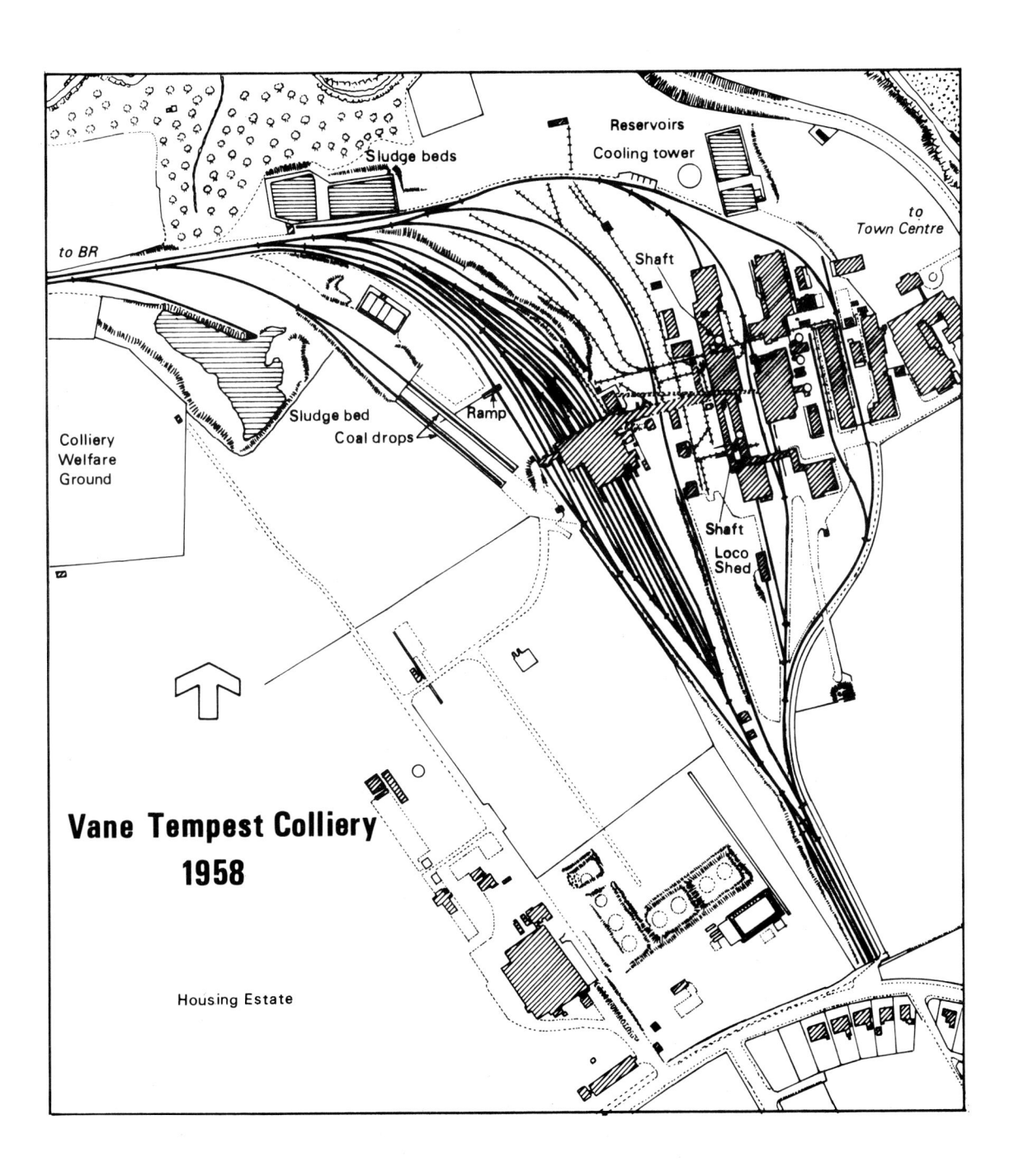

British Railways class Q6 0-8-0 number 63409 arrives from the south with a lengthy train of empty coal hoppers for Vane Tempest, on 10th August 1966. *(R.N. Pritchard)*

Operating tender-first, class K1 2-6-0 number 62007 enters the exchange sidings at Vane Tempest with empties from the north, on 10th August 1966. Sister loco 62005 is now preserved at the North Yorkshire Moors Railway. *(R.N. Pritchard)*

63409 and guards van waiting to leave the exchange sidings at Vane Tempest after bringing in the empties shown in the photograph opposite. Locomotive 63395 of this class has been preserved and can be seen at the North Yorkshire Moors Railway. *(R.N. Pritchard)*

Hawthorn Leslie 3055 of 1914 shunts Vane Tempest Colliery yard on 9th October 1964. She was sold for scrap in August 1966. *(B. Webb)*

Hawthorn Leslie 3056 of 1914, an attractive 16 inch locomotive, alongside Vane Tempest loco shed on 20th July 1968. She is now preserved at Beamish Museum. *(H.A. Gamble)*

Hawthorn Leslie 3056 propels the empties brought by British Railways class K1 2-6-0 62007 (page 80, lower) towards Vane Tempest mine, on 10th August 1966.
(R.N. Pritchard)

Manning Wardle 2036, seen here at Lambton Staithes, Sunderland, in June 1952, later worked at Vane Tempest before being transferred to Blackhall Colliery. *(F. Jones)*

CASTLEREAGH (Andrew Barclay 1885 of 1926) in steam at Vane Tempest Colliery on 22nd May 1957. The name was another of the courtesy titles of the Londonderry family. Note the lamp mounted on the cab back. *(L.G. Charlton)*

Robert Stephenson 4112 of 1935 was delivered new to Vane Tempest Colliery. She was transferred to the Lambton Railway, Philadelphia in August 1960 and scrapped there in January 1964. *(collection F. Jones)*

'Austerity' GAMMA (Bagnall 2779 of 1945) outside the loco shed on 9th May 1978, in blue livery with red coupling rods and yellow/black buffer beams. She is now preserved at the Tanfield Railway, Marley Hill, Tyne & Wear. *(A.J. Booth)*

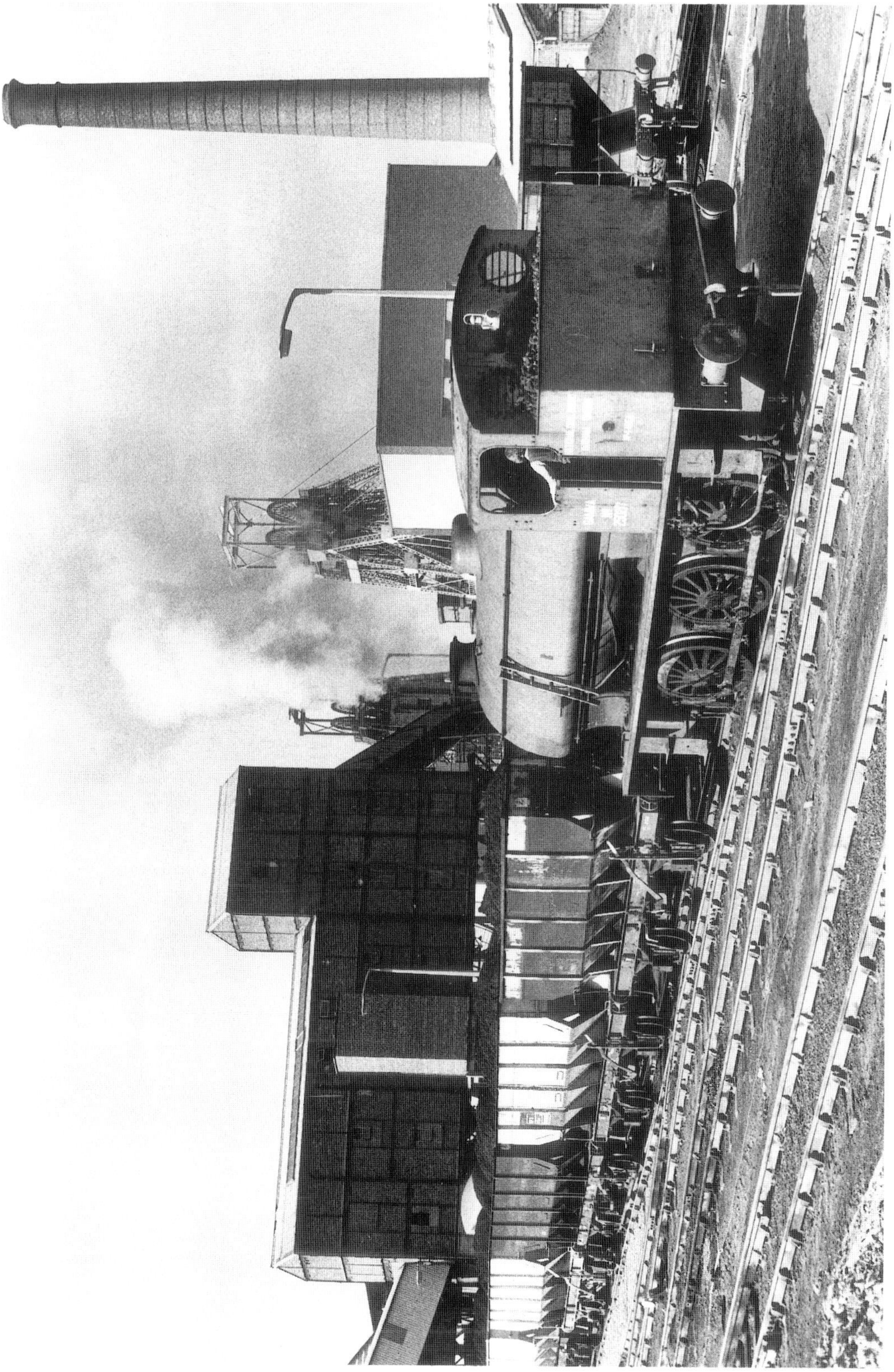

ABOVE: The crew of Bagnall 2779 keep watch as British Railways class 37 diesel number 37045 leaves with loaded coal hoppers on 28th August 1974. *(G.T. Heavyside)*

LEFT: GAMMA No.2502/7 (Bagnall 2779 of 1945) makes a fine sight shunting loaded coal hoppers at Vane Tempest Colliery on 28th August 1974. *(G.T. Heavyside)*

Bagnall 2779 on 28th August 1974. After a complete repaint she proceeded (bunker first) on 14th August 1975 along the BR line to Seaham Station, with BR inspector Quinn aboard, thence routed Hartlepool and Darlington bound for Shildon and the 'Stockton & Darlington 150' celebrations. Unfortunately, she ran hot en-route and was forced to complete her journey by low loader, although still taking her place in the cavalcade.
(G.T. Heavyside)

A general view of the Vane Tempest Colliery headgears on 9th May 1978. Narrow gauge tubs can just be glimpsed below the end of the conveyor (centre). *(A.J. Booth)*

Opposite view of the headgears, from the seaward side, showing the area fenced off with demolition works in progress. 16th January 1994. *(A.J. Booth)*

General view of the coal drops at Vane Tempest Colliery on 9th May 1978, with five hoppers in the charge of Andrew Barclay 547. *(A.J. Booth)*

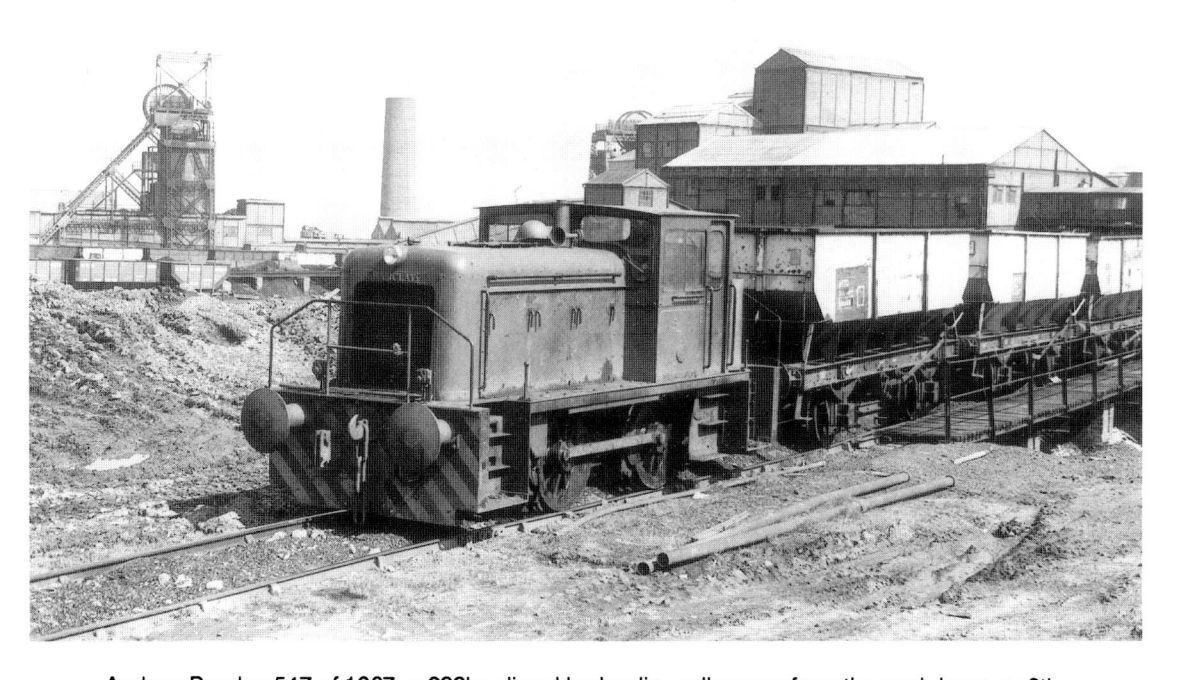

Andrew Barclay 547 of 1967, a 233hp diesel hydraulic, pulls away from the coal drops on 9th May 1978. Green livery, with red coupling rods and yellow/black buffer beams.
(A.J. Booth)

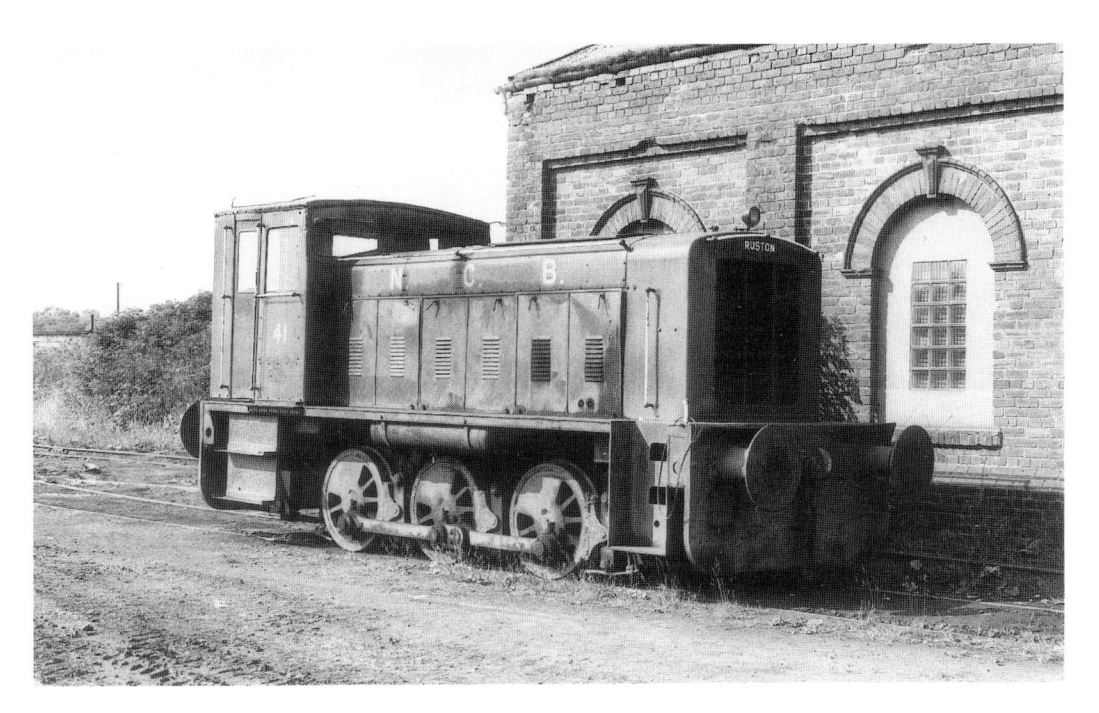

Ruston & Hornsby 421438, a class 165DE with BTH electrical equipment, standing outside the loco shed on 3rd August 1983. It was in blue livery with red coupling rods and buffer beams. Note the shed windows. *(A.J. Booth)*

The brick built locomotive shed at Vane Tempest on 13th June 1988, with the doors swung open to reveal Hunslet 6662 lurking inside. It was the last loco at this pit and left for scrapping on 21st February 1992. *(A.J. Booth)*

appendix 1
SEAHAM HARBOUR DOCK Co. LTD.
STEAM LOCOMOTIVES
(in year of construction order)

number	name	type	cylinders		builder	works number	year
3	DAWDON	0-6-0	IC	?	TR	254	1855
-	AJAX	0-6-0	IC	?	B & T	-	1867
18	-	0-6-0ST	OC	15"	BH	32	1867
16	-	0-4-0VBT	VC	?	HW	21	1870
19	-	0-4-0ST	OC	9"	BH	203	1871
17	-	0-4-0VBT	OC	?	HW	33	1873
-	MARS	0-6-0ST	IC	15"	RS	2238	1875
-	CLIO	0-6-0	IC	?	Ghd	-	1875
-	MILO	0-6-0ST	IC	15"	RS	2241	1875
18	-	0-4-0WT	OC	9"	Lewin	-	1877
-	REX	0-4-0ST	OC	10"	MW	838	1885
-	DICK	0-4-0ST	OC	10"	HE	628	1895
1	SEATON	0-6-0T	IC	?	Seaham	-	1902
-	SEAHAM	0-6-0ST	OC	14"	P	1052	1905
-	SILKSWORTH	0-6-0ST	OC	15"	P	1083	1906
44	-	0-6-0T	OC	17"	MW	1934	1917
No.1	-	0-4-0ST	OC	16"	HL	3354	1918
No.3	-	0-4-0ST	OC	16"	HL	3355	1918
10	-	0-4-0ST	OC	16"	HL	3352	1918
B No 10	-	0-4-0ST	OC	14"	HL	3476	1920
B No 38	-	0-4-0ST	OC	16"	HL	3496	1921
-	JUNO	0-6-0ST	OC	16"	HL	3527	1922
B No 23	-	0-4-0ST	OC	16"	HL	3744	1929
-	NEPTUNE	0-6-0ST	OC	16"	HL	3898	1936
B No 15	-	0-4-0ST	OC	16"	HL	3873	1936
173	-	0-4-0ST	OC	16"	HL	3919	1937
B No 41	-	0-4-0ST	OC	16"	RSH	7016	1940
177	-	0-4-0ST	OC	16"	RSH	7036	1940
52	-	0-4-0ST	OC	16"	RSH	7340	1946
24	-	0-4-0ST	OC	16"	RSH	7342	1947
25	-	0-4-0ST	OC	16"	RSH	7345	1947
54	-	0-4-0ST	OC	16"	RSH	7346	1947
183	-	0-4-0ST	OC	16"	RSH	7347	1947
-	SENTINEL	4wVBT	VCG	200hp	S	9575	1954
-	TEMPEST	4wVBT	VCG	200hp	S	9618	1956
-	-	4wVBT	VCG	200hp	S	9619	1957

DIESEL LOCOMOTIVES

number	RE number	type	hp		builder	works number	year
-	-	4wDH	308		TH	104c	1960
D1	1504/53	0-6-0DH	305		EEV	D1191	1967
D2	1506/53	0-6-0DH	305		EEV	D1192	1967
D3	1446/53	0-6-0DH	305		EEV	D1193	1967
D4	1443/53	0-6-0DH	305		EEV	D1194	1967
D5	1469/53	0-6-0DH	305		EEV	D1195	1967

appendix 2
SEAHAM COLLIERIES STEAM LOCOMOTIVES
(in year of construction order)

number	name	type	cylinders	builder	works number	year	worked at
36	-	0-4-0ST	OC 14"	P	615	1896	VT. Se.
81	SEAHAM	0-4-0ST	OC 14"	HL	2701	1907	Da.
32	-	0-4-0ST	OC 15"	HL	2826	1910	VT.
12	-	0-4-0ST	OC 16"	HL	2789	1912	Da.
24	-	0-6-0ST	OC 15"	AB	1321	1913	Se.
13	-	0-4-0ST	OC 16"	HL	3055	1914	VT.
14	-	0-4-0ST	OC 16"	HL	3056	1914	VT. Se. Da.
11	-	0-4-0ST	OC 16"	HC	1412	1920	Da.
43	-	0-4-0ST	OC 16"	GR	769	1920	Se.
82	DAWDON No.2	0-4-0ST	OC 14"	HL	3492	1921	Da.
83	LONDONDERRY	0-4-0ST	OC 14"	AB	1724	1922	Se.
48	-	0-4-0ST	OC 15"	HL	3544	1923	Se.
49	-	0-4-0ST	OC 15"	MW	2035	1924	Da.
50	-	0-4-0ST	OC 15"	MW (LEW	2036 rebuild	1924 1957)	VT.
84	CASTLEREAGH	0-4-0ST	OC 14"	AB	1885	1926	VT. Se.
85	VANE TEMPEST	0-6-0ST	OC 16"	RS	4112	1935	VT.
86	STEWART	0-4-0ST	OC 14"	AB	2160	1943	Se.
87	WYNYARD	0-4-0ST	OC 14"	AB	2165	1944	Da. VT.
2502/7	GAMMA	0-6-0ST	IC 18"	WB	2779	1945	VT.
60	-	0-6-0ST	IC 18"	HE	3686	1948	Da.
37	-	0-4-0ST	OC 15"	RSH	7755	1953	Da.
38	-	0-4-0ST	OC 15"	RSH	7756	1953	VT. Se.

appendix 3
SEAHAM COLLIERIES DIESEL LOCOMOTIVES
STANDARD GAUGE
(in year of construction order)

number	plant number	type	hp	builder	works number	year	worked at
-	-	4wPM	?	MH	L116	1939	SWW.
XL5	-	4wDM	?	LEW	-	1955	SWW.
41	9207/5	0-6-0DE	155	RH	421438	1958	VT.
8D	2307/56	0-6-0DM	204	HE	5303	1958	Da.
2	2307/55	0-6-0DM	310	AB	423	1958	Da.
10D	2309/57	0-6-0DM	204	HE	5304	1959	Se. Da.
-	-	4wDH	178	TH	105v	1962	Se.
-	05200/100	4wDM	85	MR	5766	1963	SWW.
-	20.110.703	0-4-0DH	325	RR	10201	1964	Se. VT.
-	2120/210	0-6-0DH	311	HE	6618	1965	Da.
-	9106/66	0-6-0DH	311	HE	6662	1966	VT. Se.
65	9101/65	0-6-0DH	305	EEV	D1121	1966	Se.
-	2120/211	0-6-0DH	311	AB	514	1966	VT.
-	2333/241	0-4-0DH	233	AB	523	1967	Se. Da.
-	2333/242	0-4-0DH	233	AB	524	1967	Se. Da.
-	2336/289	0-4-0DH	233	AB	547	1967	VT.
-	05080/85	0-4-0DH	233	AB	548	1967	Se. Da.
-	05200/92	0-4-0DH	233	AB	550	1968	Se.
71	2100/522	0-6-0DH	400	AB	585	1973	Se. Da. VT.
-	20.110.997	0-6-0DH	400	AB	594	1974	Da.
-	20.110.704	0-6-0DH	400	AB	603	1976	Se.
-	20.110.708	0-6-0DH	400	AB	609	1976	Da.
-	20.110.709	0-6-0DH	400	AB	613	1977	Da.
-	20.110.736	0-6-0DH	400	AB	623	1978	Se.
-	20.110.739	0-6-0DH	400	AB	624	1978	Da.
-	20.110.733	0-6-0DH	400	AB	646	1979	Da.
-	20.123.464	0-6-0DH	400	AB	659	1982	Se. VT.
-	20.123.465	0-6-0DH	400	AB	660	1982	Se.

appendix 4
SEAHAM COLLIERIES DIESEL AND BATTERY LOCOMOTIVES
SURFACE NARROW GAUGE
(in year of construction order)

name	plant number	type	hp	builder	works number	year	worked at
-	2216/261	4wBE	35	Atlas	2458	1945	Se.
-	2203/341	0-4-0DM	65	HE	3524	1947	STC.
-	2403/50	0-4-0DM	70	HE	4109	1952	STC.
-	2403/51	0-4-0DM	70	HE	4110	1952	Da.
-	2644/41	4wDM	48	RH	268873	1952	STC.
-	2216/282	0-6-0DM	100	HC	DM804	1952	Da.
-	2203/342	0-4-0DM	65	HE	4631	1953	STC.
-	2203/343	0-4-0DM	65	HE	4632	1953	STC.
VICTORIA	2216/286	0-6-0DM	100	HC	DM842	1954	STC.
-	2201/262	0-6-0DM	100	HC	DM852	1954	STC.
-	-	0-4-0DM	65	HE	4685	1955	Da.
-	05080/97	0-4-0DM	65	HE	4805	1956	Da.
TYNESIDE GEORGE	2305/54	0-6-0DM	100	HC	DM1119	1958	STC.
-	2207/456	4wBE	64	EE	2476	1958	STC.
-	2103/35	4wBE	64	EE	2519	1958	STC.
-	2203/345	0-6-0DM	100	HC	DM1065	1959	STC.
-	2201/265	0-6-0DM	100	HC	DM1169	1960	STC.
HELEN	2203/348	0-6-0DM	100	HC	DM1247	1961	STC.
-	2407/80	0-4-0DM	70	HE reb HE	5596 6620	1961 1969	STC.
-	2304/67	0-6-0DM	100	HC	DM1366	1965	STC.
-	9307/57	0-4-0DM	66	HE	6619	1966	STC.
-	05100/121	4w-4wDH	216	HE	7099	1973	STC.
LAURA	20/190/6	4wDM	60	HE	6348	1975	STC.
-	20.108.625	4w-4wDH	300	(HE (AB	8514 650	1980 1980	STC.
-	20.122.514	4w-4wDH	300	(HE (AB	8515 651	1981 1981	STC.
-	20.110.050	4wBE	17½	CE	B3464A	1988	STC.

note: narrow gauge flameproof locos also worked underground at Dawdon and Vane Tempest collieries.

INDUSTRIAL RAILWAY SOCIETY

The Industrial Railway Society, which was formed in 1949 as the Industrial Locomotive Information Section of the Birmingham Locomotive Club, caters for enthusiasts interested in privately owned locomotives and railways. Members receive the INDUSTRIAL RAILWAY RECORD, a profusely illustrated magazine; a bi-monthly bulletin containing topical news and amendments to the Society's Handbook Series; access to a well-stocked library; visits to and rail tours of industrial railway systems; a book sales service; loco information service from the Society's team of records officers; photograph sales service; and access to archives held at the NRM, York. Further details are available by sending a stamped addressed envelope to:

Bernard Mettam, 27 Glenfield Crescent, Newbold, Chesterfield S41 8SF.

Subscriptions to the INDUSTRIAL RAILWAY RECORD are available to non-members of the Society. Enquiries regarding subscriptions and back numbers should be addressed to:

R.V. Mulligan, Owls Barn, The Chestnuts, Aylesbeare, Exeter, Devon EX5 2BY.

Seaham as it is fondly remembered. June 1965. *(C.T. Gifford)*